Reviewing the Skull

Also by Judy Rowe Michaels

Dancing with Words: How To Help Students Love Language

The Forest of Wild Hands: Poems

Risking Intensity: Writing And Reading Poetry with High School Students

Reviewing the Skull

Poems

Judy Rowe Michaels

WordTech Editions

Cover image: "Sharps!" © 2000, John Magnan. Photo: Tim
Sylvia, New Bedford, Massachusetts

Published by WordTech Editions
P.O. Box 541106
Cincinnati, OH 45254-1106

ISBN: 9781934999790
LCCN: 2009942290

Poetry Editor: Kevin Walzer
Business Editor: Lori Jareo

Visit us on the web at www.wordtechweb.com

Grateful acknowledgements to the editors in whose publications these poems, sometimes in altered versions, first appeared:

"Morning at the Irish Coffee House" and "Cancer Muse" have appeared in *U.S. 1 Worksheets.*
"In Remission?" appeared in *Kalliope* as a finalist in the Sue Saniel Elkind Poetry Contest.
"To Picasso's *Melancholy Woman*" appeared in *Ekphrasis.*
"Ghostkill" appeared in *Lips.*
"Recurrence Suite" and "The Quilters of Gee's Bend" won honorable mention in the *Nimrod*/Hardman Pablo Neruda Prize competition. "Saint Luke's Garden, Hudson Street" was a finalist in *Nimrod's* contest.
"Advent Lambs" appeared in *Thatchwork: Delaware Valley Poets.*

I appreciate John Magnan's generosity in allowing me to use his sculpture "Sharps!" for my cover.

I am grateful to the MacDowell Colony, the Banff Centre for the Arts, the Geraldine R. Dodge Foundation, the New Jersey State Council on the Arts, and Princeton Day School for invaluable gifts of time and funding. Special thanks to Baron Wormser and each of the Cool Women, who have offered careful readings of many of these poems, and especially to Lois Harrod, who handled the formatting of the manuscript. Thanks also to poet friends Patricia Hooper, Rita Pappas and Chris Cunningham. And deep gratitude always for the wisdom and patient support of my sister poet, Terry Blackhawk, and my husband, Bill Michaels, who bring equal measures of precision and profundity to their reading of my poems.

For Ellen, Chris, Tim, Randy

Contents

3.

I dreamt I was all bones;
The dead slept in my sleeve.

—*Theodore Roethke*

I

Cancer Muse

What they don't know is

she's my mother, come back from
beyond the frame. You're writing too much
about breath, she says, plucking

a dismissive minor chord. Anyone would think
a body never breathed before. I want to
remind her it was good enough

for Emily, with her
zero at the bone,
which is what I'm afraid of, but

I can't tell my mother, she knows too much–
the sigh, the gasp, the final catch–
and she's not telling. Self-reliance,

she breathes into me, along my
nerves. Your breath will take
care of itself, so give your mind

to harder things, like laughter.
I want to say, How do you think
it feels when I dream your death

is mine? No–please don't turn
away. I need to know what happened
when I left you. Most nights I get this far:

flat pillow, you struggling for breath, your face
the wraith of mine. Your voice
rasps in my throat. The morphine pump

is mine, too, and the desperate trust
in strangers. But were you
ready? How could you bear to stop,

well, breathing? Who else can I ask?
Don't look like that. Of course I haven't
grown up. No, it doesn't just

take care of itself. When I last kissed
your forehead, I thought tomorrow would
wait for you. I live your nights

often. The sudden lights, needles, smells
are mine, too, but morning always comes,
so far. I'm still learning to breathe.

Some laughter skims the sea
a long time before diving. In your last year
breath came hard, laughter

sounded tight. Your ashes
spell no answer. You never
showed me tears, until I touched your face

at last, and even then—Oh, the bright
air inside this frame, despite
infection. So bright I can't begin

to tell you what you've lost.

To Picasso's *Melancholy Woman*

I want to sink into the deep-blue shadow
that falls across your cheek as you turn away
from us and the window, your throat funneling dark
heavier blue into shoulders that carry sorrow
down to the chest's concavity. Let me
hide where the gathered blue finally
goes black–in your lap. Empty madonna,
you cradle melancholy, but its shapeless weight
spills out of the frame.
              My fear's distilled
to one dark spot so small, under the x-ray's blue,
it tells us nothing yet but *watchful waiting*. Almost
what you and I do here, you nursing
at invisible breasts some loss
not even your painter knows, that can't
grow less or deeper than the paint allows.
All you can do is watch for me to give
your pooled blues the weight of mortal fear.

Introducing the Skull

Day before Easter Break, I introduce
the skull–a young woman's. She'd hung, lissome
and lightly swaying, deep in a closet
of the bio lab. Delicately I beheaded her,
admiring the wired, polished jaw
eternally expectant. I tried to forget
the bone saw that must have cut the twin
concavities which I hold now in either hand
and bring together, front to back, a match
perfect as her missing lips. Carefully
I take her down the hall to English XII
and set her on the floor, her eye sockets
dry and pointless.
               "Hey, guys,"
the soccer captain jokes, "it's staring right at Jeff.
He'll be the first to go." I tell them how John Donne
tried sleeping in his coffin. How Golgotha
meant place of the skulls. Two girls admit
that knowing it's a woman creeps them out—
no face, no hair, but this was, like, her mind
we're trying not to look at. . . how does she feel,
naked with strangers. . . where have her thoughts gone?
Finally a boy ventures close, gingerly lifts
the two halves into his lap, runs a finger
over the forehead, "So small," remembers
"a soft spot there when you're born, the whatsit,
fontanel." And the skull is passed around,
except one girl turns away, in tears, says we're being
disrespectful. "No, really, it's okay," a guy reaches over,
gives her a little hug, "she must have left
her body to science. She'd want us
to touch."

18

It's quiet now,
the skull back on the floor. Our circled desks
make it almost cozy, a dying campfire, or maybe
some familiar relic, known since childhood,
still emanating light. The color's a cross
between khaki and old ivory–*bone,* my mother
called it, shade of those Easter shoes that pinched.
I flick from face to face, knowing the hour's
almost up, but now, bent over notebooks,
they make me think of lilies, heavy-headed
hanging from frail stalks.
                And some strange warmth's
releasing scents they didn't know they had.

Spring Outburst

On tiptoe to sniff lilac—
two wings and a heart
burst out of the bush.
Rhythm of God, this Sunday radio's
phrase for a jazz sermon, call
and response, though you
don't see the shrub's on fire with
flight when you thrust into its
purple business.
                  Rhythms of God,
when a cell sparks and booms, renewing
last spring's tumor, miniature Nagasaki,
the cloud opened like a fiery flower
and birds came tumbling down.

Not simple as inhale
exhale, body of spring you're
born with. A bomb's tucked up
inside your head.
If it doesn't call, why do you answer?
The mind's intent, hungry
for patterns, for heartbeat.
Will the lilac
explode this time? Opaque
its purple script, and the bird
already gone.

Jazz Sister

for Ellen

Okay, I understand about the groove:
the pluck, the pedal, the hush hush whisper of skins,
the thud flick flick thud regular as morning
coffee–after all, we grew up with the same
mother, tuna casserole every week–and those
left-hand chords that keep to themselves,
pretend they don't know what the hell your right
hand is thinking.

And I kind of get the scales–too arbitrary if you were
in at Creation and heard all the pitches flying free as a mad cat,
but still, music needs syntax to jazz with,
though we poets like the blue notes best.

What throws me, what makes me wonder how you
got some gene I missed out on so you marinate
salmon in maple syrup and make it
taste good–what mystifies me is
the hummingbird stuff,
that improv.

You do this in public?

It's Double Dutch. I never figured out
how to jump into those two ropes crossing,
with both ears being sawed in half by
don't forget the red hot
pepper.
      I have to go off to some rock at the end of the world
and get my poems before dawn, so even the sun

can't watch.

But you just walk on stage and arc and dive down into the lily's
throat, or hover, invisible beat of wings on the blue edge
of time, a tease, a meditation, a chromatic fall
into sugar,
        cupping silence with a syncopation.

It's courage music, that says anything
is possible, fluke, flinch, sharp, flat,
slow dance up the mountain,
maples to birch to pine, deep woods
or a sudden clearing.
        You play
the light and shadow as they fall.

Morning at the Irish Coffee House

Kathleen lies halfway across the chessboard,
stretching her arms to gather in queens, horses,
king's men. She pulls them to her heart
as a grown woman might embrace sun-warmed
sheets from the line. At play her brothers had dickered,
offering deals, sacrifices, new rules. But I want to know
what Kathleen knew as she sat watching,
hugged softly by a sweater of pale pink fleece,
thumb in her mouth. You could almost hear
the birds tuning up in her mind,
but was this waking or falling into sleep?
Her eyes are as quiet as stones beneath
water whose blue is a miraculous gloss
on the hidden. If pawns and kings are
equally desirable, why play when you could
sweep them all into your lap, so many
apples or buttons or thumbs or stars
that grow warm if you merely
go on breathing?

*

So do you feel older, Kathleen?
You must have grown in your sleep,
the waiter in green sweats says
to the owner's little girl, who gazes
dreamily at some long, pale blue
scarves for sale in the hall.
There are Celtic signs and cushions,
lace at the windows and a birthday
already moving into twilight
behind the lace. The young man's voice

drops lightly on Kathleen's red curls.
I can hear him growing
toward father, his laugh is soft
and falls from a long way up
like watered silk I could
wrap around my bare shoulders,
blue silk to dream in, deepening
like an easy chair, a wing chair
in the livingroom where father
sits late in the evenings. I could hear
their conversation, low and intimate,
if I crept through the upstairs dark
to lean out over the landing, when I
couldn't fall asleep. So do you feel
older? This morning sunlight is a firm
hand pulling back the curtains, while Kathleen
smiles, very quiet with the scarves.

On the Long Island RR, Ronkonkoma Line, Reading Your Last Interview

for Kenneth Koch, with gratitude for *Rose, where did you get that red?*

And I underscore your words, in a fever,
anything—*necktie, fire escape, irrevocably
blue, marijuana, guided missile,
postmature, onions*—we can't stop your
dying, the furling of syllable
and vine. If we try to go back,
musk, Olivetti, image and *spinach,*
we won't be the same, no first-time
vivre or joie, no boats, no madrigal
behind walls. In the next seat a father
asks the small boy if he remembers
all seven dwarves—*lumpy, bumpy,
stumpy,* he says, laughter and bounce.
The mind begs to trap in ivory,
amber, jelly, ink, your fleet voice, no time
for particle or the fuss and fling of
preposition. It was May,
you had a month left, *celebration,
leukemia, cliff, orgasm, Wittgenstein*
saying there are no subjects in the world.
But elsewhere?
              We pitch our tents just for the night, *bottle
neck, corkscrew,* then send the secret out to
sea. Shade your eyes, sleep on it.
Behind me the small boy reading aloud
bird, egg   tweet,   his lips
kiss the word and part.

Brothers And Sisters

for my parents

North for Christmas, we find ourselves grown small,
        enough to slip back
                into the old books.
They have waited, closed and cold, for the first fumbling
        key in the lock, for flames
to be coaxed from split birch, for us to remember
        how we'd peel bark to write on, secretly
                baring the smooth, pinkgold flesh.

Our first night we are mature, reading the news,
though wood smoke and mother's cold pajamas
        still hanging from a peg
                rock us part way home.
But after the next night's dishes, one of us
        drifts to a shelf, helpless,
                hovering on the verge of sleep,

and opens slowly to a picture– Toad in goggles
and motorcar. Or the bridge of crocodiles,
        each licking the pink lollipop stuck
                on the next one's tail.
Here is a kind of terror: If we take the book down
        out of the shadowy corner into the light,
                will there be sleep

or waking, and which is best? We know now
that towers fall and parents change and none of us
        turned into parents, which sometimes seems as strange
                as caterpillars smoking,

or as the way mind blurs, like the caves we made in sheets,
   reading late
      till the flashlight wavers, falls, the billowy white
        collapses on the page

and we lie still, like you, two voices
I almost hear in the walls, shiver of dying light
    that flares whenever one of us becomes
        Mole or Rat on the riverbank.
Daylight brings clarity of chores, a shared
inheritance of wood and water, though we sense
   like a late remembered dream
      more change under the cold.

Birdwriting

on stone

      over water spilling on stone

          a beaky moment   *chip*
                wing tip   *entrails*

Today at the falls I try to read a robin's skitter.

In Latin, the hero's undetermined mind translates: *moving swiftly*
   now one way, now another. But always he has to arrive

                        somewhere.

To bathe? To drink? To flee? The claws raking
warm rock, breaking lines that lead, finally,
nowhere. My head flicks with his.   Birdwriting again.

Once, in wet sand   the sea gull's feet

    I'd been cut open, drugged, scarred, slowed
    to a phrase   weeping because

the prints looked like small umbrellas.

Today I watch the bird's breast swell, subside, swell,
frail in the canyon rock   my heart tries
closing against half-thoughts
               of being

entered once more, the tumor's silent ways

      each day's tiniest ache
a sign?   Birdwriting holds it at bay
    won't let the sentence   in

Climbing Eagle Crag

for my parents

If I went alone to a grave,
took leave, year after year, with a single
flower–would loss grow clear

that way, distilled sharp as names
in stone? They chose ashes
flung in air. Each summer now, we four–

uneasy but together– climb for hours
along a brook, through hemlock,
over granite and blueberry, to find

the edge where each of us can feel
singly. Dread? Hurt?
Desire? Fear of saying nothing

or too much. Years ago
we learned the sharp, clear cry
that brings your own voice back to you

from the air. You had to be
shameless, high-pitched, sure
of getting a return. For just that moment

concentrated as rock,
surrounded but alone, I could
make distance speak.

II

The Quilters of Gee's Bend

for Donna

So many ways of fading into beauty, washedblue
waterygrayblue lavender worn down worn out all but the pocket
linings where denim's still bright, unrubbed by hands that thrust
outward over and over toward cotton ripened under
raw sun, unsparing light that washes
head scarves, work pants, straight ahead eyes, so many
ways of fading, pucker and shrink, rusty blood's
counterpoint on the beatdown stripes of a mattress,
so many ways of crossing over, of coming home.
We wasted nothing, there wasn't nothing to waste.
A bend in the Alabama, living three sides to water,
one road out. *We lived a hard starvation life*
but we didn't know it. We were all poor, so nobody
laughed at nobody else. They hung their quilts
on the line and fadebright patches flashed as far
as the highway, tired pink of a child's raggly dress
wavered halfway down her daddy's turned out bluejean
pockets, snugged up to the quilter's green print Sunday
best still full of flames and hymns and sweat
of close-pressed bodies swaying.

New York, post-Christmas:
line around the block, sidewalk coffee
in gloved hands, minimal whining,
we've seen the *Times*, we crave
the downhome warmth of folk
art, jazzy strip and patch
of waste not want not, exotic as
raw cotton, as work by
oil lamp, as motherdaughter
hand-me-down thimble,

as a women's circle
piecing, singing, praying.
Our secret present to us—
art against odds, this
long forgotten beauty
pulled off the line.

You and I go back some forty, no, more like fifty
years, unlikely friendship, puckered, faded,
you the artist, seamstress, telling me after we hug
under the museum's Calder mobile
that you once tried quilting but it was pesky,
persnickety work, those tiny, endless
stitches. And then in the third room here's Loretta
Petway's color slashes hanging over her
words, she didn't want to sew, not after fifty miles
walking the cotton, then taking care of a man and kids,
but cold nights at home they needed covers.

   Without your eye, I might have missed
this narrow flowered binding that runs out
of one fabric and turns blithely into another,
the crinkles and uneven sides shrunk from too much
washing, contrasts of worn blue knees and brighter
pockets, blend of art and desperation.

   Slow walking wears us out. We reach the video
halfway through and silently stay on to catch
the start. You like the way I'm scribbling words,
colors, stripes, in random corners of my bankbook
for later. I like it when you tell me how this quilt
reminds you of your mother, her fashions that tried for
daring but never quite broke free.

In a room almost of her own, Annie Mae's quilts
tug at us from every wall. She says she wants
color that takes her attention away from everything.

They plastered their walls with newspapers for heat.
Sometimes you'd be looking at them and suddenly
you'd see something could go in a quilt.
She kept away from the other women. She tore
instead of cut. *Sometimes a quilt came right*
into my mind.

      I read her, wondering
if you paused, too. If you felt
dazzled? You stood here, didn't
call me over, saw whatever you saw
alone. I guess that's how we learn
to make things. For years I'd cut
along the dotted lines, while your cloth ricocheted
under the needle of some wild machine.
Either way, no children.
And then the deaths set in.
Now sometimes a door
flares open with no wind, and I'm dazed–
a piece of your past making sense of mine.
I touch the long, fringed scarf you've made me,
wrapped twice about my throat, the soft wool
deeply striped so many different blues
my eyes match one of them.

Before we leave, I go back to the first quilt I
stopped at and the maker's words recorded
by Missouri, her daughter–*I'm going to take*
his work clothes and shape them into a quilt
to remember him, and cover up
under it for love.

Last Visit

I recognize the man on the other end
of the leash. We all three
get off at the cancer floor and I know
whose love has summoned this dog.
I've seen his picture in her room here
and on the wall a calendar
of Bernese Mountain dogs, strong for work
or love. I've read about him in her poems,
the puppy meant to be her sick boy's
friend, who at Sam's death walked the fields
with her. Who came to know
a hand's unsteadiness on the leash.
His fur must have caught and held her tears
like Sam's soft flannel quilt.

The dog is led away into a darkened room
where last things now are first.
The family's gathered, so I stay outside.
Perhaps someone will lift her hand
and bury it in the familiar coat—
so beautiful, the black and brown and white
separate but blended, and the wet, black nose
that used to point her home.

At Home

His watercolors cover the walls.
She says, "It wasn't a nice death."
The winter sky bleeds gray to lavender.
Some days the earth's a hospital.

She says it wasn't a nice death.
She lets me choose a watercolor.
Some days the earth's a hospital.
Dream right, and snow freezes the ground.

She lets me choose a watercolor:
Pines and shore seem to float.
Dream right, and snow freezes the ground.
I have what he died of.

Pines and shore seem to float,
he left the very bottom white.
I have what he died of.
He chose to come home.

Harry Partch: *Bitter Music*

The way of music is money, for instruments, and for a place to
live to keep and repair them; and what is even harder, it
is the way of people to play them whose souls are in tune with
the expresser's.
　　　Harry Partch, 1935

Always on the edge: tonight
you lie under the wild lilac tree
high on a crumbling cliff
that holds you from the sea's
eradications as from a deathly
hypnotizing music
played by unbending men in
tight black suits.
The hills ascend–*arpeggios*,
you scribble. Your other hand
feeds an oily eucalyptus fire.
A hobo's at the saucer edge of life,
but fire brings him back to center.
Musicians should know how to tune their instruments
as a bum tends a fire
with his breath.
Keyboards to you are cracks between the notes.
Hands with a mere five fingers? Sheriffs,
railway police, citizens who screw
their mouths up tight at panhandlers.

You stick a thumb out,
clean sewers, sleep naked
in haystacks, and then come home
to hobo camp to hear the male music,
men on the skids between the sharps and flats.
You notate self-pity on a sliding scale

unknown to government–
at least a sign the ego's still alive.
Your nickname in the camps
"Blue Monday"–from sullen harmonies
of curses, animal jokes, and booze.
On the road the need to beg
sticks in your craw *like tight-assed octaves.*
In camp the rumor goes they put an "eroscide"
in the nightly stew to kill desire.

   When I was six, I drew a stallion
   all correct, the organ long and portentous.
   A little girl hit me hard, then she re-drew
   the belly to her liking.
          There are men to love,
unshaven dipsos, gentle but full-voiced.
You built a rainbow organ, forty-three notes
to the scale, over two hundred different-colored tones.
How to explain? I give music away
that people haven't yet grown ears for.
This is the fourteenth house whose steps you've climbed,
a homeless please-eyes dog. At last, two cans–
pea soup and condensed milk.
And a lighted cigarette tossed from a car.
Some critic said Yeats can't carry a tune,
can't tell one note from another. The poet said,
 "I hear a more ancient music."

Your present task's to shield this cigarette
and hear the sea wind fingering the cliff.

All quotations are taken from *Bitter Music* by Harry Partch (edited
by Thomas McGeary, University of Illinois Press, 1991).

Recurrence

Won't meet my eyes, doesn't offer his hand,
jaw's locked down grim as a TV surgeon's.
My return has marked me *failure*.
Only two years ago that hand, gloved,
was probing me for tumor every month,
his mantra, gently, "I'm sorry, I'm sorry"
each time I flinched. Three years ago those hands
took out my ovaries, sampled tissue. Those eyes
broke the bad news to me when I woke up.
"Inoperable," he says now, heads for the door
muttering "Chemo." I block him: "Couldn't the scan
be wrong?" He pushes past. "Hell, why?
Thing lit up just like the Fourth of July."

Sharps!

sculpture by John Magnan: pine, steel, walnut
at the Ovarian Cancer convention

1

Chainmail egg,
it glitters with pain.
46,000
heads of pins
he snapped off,
hammered
into the wood
and set in a bristly
nest of shearings,
fierce fallout,
pursing pins in his mouth
like a seamstress,
one hand firm on the
egg's forged armor,
bright with seeds
stillborn
from his hammer.

2

He is a sculptor, he can't help it when
disease takes her by the hand
down to the infusion room and his mind
thinks *shape, mass, line* as he watches
poison drip from the plastic bag,
thinks as the level slowly drops
convex caving in,

drip, endless drip, and the hand
of the clock must circle six times round and
he would go mad with the drip if
he couldn't dig nails into palm and
twist, carve, pound, bolt

next week he starts the egg.

3

and does she feel
do we
feel rescued
by the pain of the pins
nailing her down
in steel lamé? can his
patient rage
bring her back
to the open air,
to the nest inside
her skull
changed now
in the cancer
mirror,
like a bristlecone
burst and
come back
after fire?

Undoing the Dark

for Tim, 1951-2005

A bewilderment of fireflies:
Who's pushing buttons in tonight's
tangle of meadow and branch?
Now   and *now*
Where you are,
is it *all* now?
                 on   off   on
off   in this narrow
summer lane where I flash on you cutting
yourself, again, again,
some scars they said were five years old,
a fireflight in your mind,
                       on   off
what people saw was sparkle,
spray and spill like champagne, cascades
of wit and music.
              On the phone
your favorite phrase, "We got
a standing ovation!" My little brother
tall on the podium, baton extending your reach,
tuxedo slightly crumpled, arms flung wide
to love your audience's love, your wild bows
left, right, fired up with Beethoven.
You were fifty-three and cutting
your chest, they would find knives, arrows,
daggers at the scene, a couple
of guns in the car, they said "bizarre"
and I flashed on Bernini's
arrows of light, Theresa, ecstatic pain,
but that was suffering faith,

43

made beautiful for our admiration.
We are not saints.
                    The music
sustained you for a time
with its desperate tests—
leap, plunge, lift.
With its momentary deaths.
You took these from the page
and made them speak, but you
kept silent. And now I can't
undo the dark you've made.

In Remission?

She feels swollen, touches her belly
not like a woman with child
who's moon-ripe, riding
high and sure.
                    She has never known
such making. This is no caress,
she wants to push, press, beat down,
knead out
                    the white tumescence.

Huge in the desert air, a moon
leaps at her, bloated omen
of something her fingers fear
to palpate, mystery buried
deep as a fetus.

Is it a witchy power
to raise again what was cut,
burned, drugged?
She has no seeds, no pouches,
her prayers run backwards gabbling towards
child, *if I should die before I wake,*
now I lay me, her prayers are fingers
addressing flesh resistant, secretive, already
hard and green.
                    They said three years.
Is the moon come round so soon?

Harp Convention

for Gwyneth

When you show me into the first chamber,
something says, Close your eyes,
and I do. Outside, air was hot enough
to shrivel a lizard. I'd been brooding
over x-rays, I was my own storm
unable to burst. Something said,
don't even let yourself
imagine.
      I cross a threshold
and the air breaks out
glissandos–a shivering glass of sounds
that wrap and fracture like light on water.
I lose all direction.
          You tell me
this is just twelve harps,
beyond are many more, this is
after all a harp convention, hundreds
of strings, pedals, sounding boards,
welling with intent and accident.

This one room is enough to hold me,
like the first time I came west, heard
the Pacific roar in the pitch of night
somewhere far below me.
Salt twist, shore bloom,
its many fingered winds,
invisible.

Whale Watch

We're all leaning over the rail, willing you
to rise again from the gray-green deeps of our longing.
Surely you can feel the tug of seventy hearts.
Enlarge our mammal lives, breathe on us, show us
only a glimpse of salt-laced flank,
we can do the rest, we can
fill our lungs for the long plunge home.

Singly, who would have felt this?
Who among us woke today with your name on our lips?
Camcorder slung from neck like an amulet,
we sampled shore delights—fudge in the shape of shells,
nose rings of whalebone, sailor hats for dogs,
but who imagined this boat of souls
stirring to point and gasp
when you spouted almost under the boat?

Yes there were guarantees, but we're all used
to scams. I expected, not a rubber fish but
the merest gray glint, a minor troubling of the waves
that I'd be sure to miss, the way I always
look in exactly the wrong part of the sky when a star
shoots.
        But you heave yourself up and loll,
generous as Walt bathing with his imagined
twenty-five beautiful young naked men, you
make me touch the shoulder of the nearest stranger,
lock eyes with him for a moment, we point wildly, dance
separate but together, and each time you rise
we all but shout:

split tail lightning   sea treader

47

fish sucker   *slickback*

wave of the wave   *boat thruster*

master of gasp and silent singing

You are better than stars. Your sudden blow
undoes the Not of our bodies
till the boat is one vast orgasm of whale,
rocking and rocked.

After the afterglow
of the long ride home, I begin to release you from
avatar, shaman, back to slime and reek,
or slow death by trash. If you could
read a human face, you'd see yourself
become an It. My face goes flat and drained
of light, bony, unpromising as a juiceless fish.

Washed up on my own strand, I sense you
shrunk and limp somewhere behind my eyes, waiting
for me to dream a place so deep and cold
that you swim up alongside, surface and breathe,
unbolt your song and give me passage.

Recurrence Suite

1

After X-rays

I am in love with the lesion on my liver,
how its quick thickening
defines the dark.
Such lèse-majesté! I love how it flies a skull and crossbones
from the heart of the mother ship.
I'm in awe of its discontent.
How did it know me across a crowded room?
I love it with sleepless nights,
I love it on alternate days,
I love it incestuously.
My secret that defies the hot, bright shower of particles,
that eludes the fumbling knives.
How it clings to its glandular host,
how it finds its way around my slippery defenses.
I am in love with its little suction cup feet,
with its mysterious past, its hunger.
I could die for its grim dividings,
for its knowledge of hidden names.

2

Biopsy

The books call it a train you're on,
and each new test a station where you
might get off and watch the fear
pick up speed, new freight,
new distances. Metaphor
is a carrier–of disease, of terror.
Yesterday the technician,
a mere girl, curly and big-eyed,
missed my vein twice. The station
was 2, or maybe 3, announced
in a foreign tongue that you almost
understand from birth, but learn
to forget. Anyway,
it made my wiring flash
what if? The current locution
is *we don't have to go there*
yet. But mind has a mind of its own,
is already there–stage 3, 4, 5–of course
it knows people who went right
to the end of the line,
and in the name of self control,
of be prepared, it's improvising
death. It remembers
the chemo nurse teaching my
mother to say *I'm buying*
some time, my mother
carrying everywhere the little green
plastic bowl to be sick in,
while her mind tried to shut up

about *quality of life,* and mine
went on celebrating in a terrible
secret refrain, *not me, not me,*
not me.

3

Waiting for News

When you wade the low tide
on a morning that is already singing
and your eyes wake more birds
high in the red-fleshed trees,
and you know for good and all
where the sure-footed, deep dance you
do with the slipping stones
comes from, how can you not
trust the dance in your cells—
kick, fire, split, die, kick.
If that is diseased, then so is
the quick-diving flow of the heron's neck,
and the breaking wave that receives him,
and the blue depth of sky
that colors my breath. These pierced
like a surgeon's needle
and found nothing but light.

4

New Surgeon

We're *all* terminally ill, my surgeon says,
his pony tail energizing the white room,
giving me numbers I was dumb enough
to ask for—*one* (shake) *to three* (shake) *years,*
three if you have the operation. No one but me
will hear this, loved ones believe in beating
the odds. From wherever lost things go
I call back *irrationals* and *imaginary*
numbers. I used to love the words, their meanings
shadowy in the brightness of sound, chiaroscuro
of the can't win, beautiful as a luna moth
betrayed by hot lights, its wings beating out
green, luminous, shriveling death. We know
in our crazed rhythms of loss and cling, oh how we
come to know, the irrational roots, how like
some shaky old jazz sideman we keep time
with all the imaginary drummers.

Waiting Again for Surgery

Somewhere near the border, Mind lost its passport,
      runs up and down corridors
            wondering what if it's stopped, stripped, searched,

suppose they find hidden papers, maybe the lost x-rays,
      the missing case chart: sixty-two-year-old white female,
            tumors, poems, Brahms, she can't remember

her ovaries, the shape of her mouth, maybe the cat's
      to blame, he's taken to stealing
         into her bed while she sleeps–

rubs, sheds, turns around three times, then forms a tight ball
      of nerves, Mind isn't sleeping well,
            wakes each hour or else dreams trips on stationary trains

across black-edged snow where a man in a powdered wig
      plays fugues on a glass harmonica and there's no
           anesthesia, each morning the cat is gone,

one night a pair of foreign agents enter the train,
      Mind tells them its suspicions, they weep,
         have to be hugged, reassured,

something got lost in translation, maybe,
      though Mind dreams now in several languages,
         hedging its bets, if stopped by border guards

it can say *fear* or *cure*, enough to get by.

Letter to My Husband

When the house caught fire last night
and I nearly burned to death before
I woke. . . while you were sailing
the rivers of Russia and ten firemen
demanded your keys to move the car
when I said, half asleep, no, he's taken
all the keys to Russia . . . and the six cats
of the (also) missing landlady shot through the door
when the biggest guy lifted his booted foot
and wood shivered, gave way. . . when at
midnight the Chief asked for my license,
all identity dissolved in smoke. . . when
the landlady finally arrived on antidepressants
smiling the one word *horrible* and they told her
five more minutes till the bags and boxes
she lived with would have caught
and then nothing could save the place. . . when
I thought about all the fires on TV and did
they, the ones on the pavement below, ever
sleep again . . . when I tried picturing you in
a boat on foreign waters in your delusion of
safety and onion domes nested in more
onion domes. . . when I knew we'd never lose
this smell of a burnt dinner we didn't eat. . . when
I suddenly feel gratitude take me in my unburned
bed. . . I wonder when dawn comes if I'll
believe it, maybe I'll just have dreamed I
was alive and will wake on fire, dying.

Ghostkill

He thought you died last summer,
she tells me, hand over the receiver,
and I know she wonders—is it safe

to laugh? She wants me tough,
wit-cracking, flicking ash at destiny.
So here's to death in the air, death

by wire, like flowers—dead a year
on an invisible someone's
breath. It doesn't feel the same

as being present at your own funeral,
which never appealed to me. No,
hearing you've died feels more like

one of those ghost squares in the family
album, where four black, gummed corners
went dry and released the snapshot

of you in a highchair or a wedding veil:
Where did it go? Like a phone voice
that doesn't know the listener's hung up.

III

After Watching a Film on Agnes Martin

The camera fills us with her quiet:
Mind waits for a painting,
empties itself of eighty years,

of cliffs slicing dry Taos air,
hawks with their bloody news.
Her back to the horizon,

she awaits the horizontals,
the measured grid that she calls
innocence. We might call it

absence. Not desert–
the other woman painted that,
white curve of bone and yucca's

creamy spiral, her studio
crammed with round.
Martin's line is straight,

though she resists the square
as too aggressive,
favors the soft rectangular.

We hear her breathing,
heavy, rough, an old body
trying not to try.

She gave up facts
except the canvas shape,
to go for infinite.

*Forty years of horizontal
lines, some kind of record.*
But each new work

is won by waiting.
Till nothing matters
more than something else,

body is field, both
immaterial, and mind's
a penciled grid.

*We're born a hundred percent
free, after that it's all
adjustment.* Her brush

starts a pale yellow wash
from the canvas edge.
It's not natural,

the band's too even,
too pure, almost invisible,
but you want her

to go on. The canvas
is big enough to step into,
but empty

of attachment, only
the grid stretching us
toward endless.

On the Tongue

I become mistress
of Early. He wakes me
with a sudden kiss
before death can
find me. *Now I lay
me down to sleep* was never
my last hope, with its
trust, its bland neutrality,
its disposable soul
offered to God for keep
or take, which sounded like
no choice at all.
        I didn't guess
I was mistress of Early
till I tried the phrase
on my tongue, and swallowed,
tasting a still-dark sky, faint
light at the edges or maybe
foreknowledge of light,
of birds stirring.
        Some call this
insomnia. But mistress of Early
is out of madrigal by unalarmed.
From under the goosedown,
Early licks my eyelids, takes me
undreaming in the dark,
while night yawns
and slowly, so far
inevitably,
gives birth
to a window of
trees.

Readying

First the large, round ears,
then a lurching shoulder
blocks the faint light between trees

on this hardnosed mountain,
and because it was hill farms once
I think, "Horse–got loose from spring plowing,"

but suddenly I know it's moose.
How did she get here?
Spring has barely climbed this far.

I'm up to open the cabin with my brothers,
claiming the place, though the lake's
too cold. Yesterday I put wild flowers

on mother's night table–Solomon's seal,
gaywing, clintonia, wintergreen,
saying their names aloud

to fill the bare room that I won't take
for mine, the air's still tangled.
Meanwhile the moose

holds us, an awkward truth
too great to see around. The trail's
hers as long as she wants it.

It's our only way down through steep rush
of trees and rock, but we'll wait till she's
ready to make her own.

At Café Mews

for my brother (1951-2005)

Dear Tim, the bar's mahogany and lined
with gorgeous men, this being Provincetown.
The angelwaves of summer sea and sails
fly just beyond the floor-to-ceiling windows.
Here's fumé blanc to you,
though you would take Bordeaux and choose
the rack of lamb. We really should come here
in winter, then I'd order red
and this same little table by the stove.
We could be cozy, just the way we were
that New Year's blizzard. Stuck in Maine
we stoked the fire, broke out the Veuve Clicquot
and grocery cake, paid full attention
to one another—not too much.

How many years before you'd take your life?

I'm eating pricey tuna here, soy-glazed
with ginger, in your honor, not
the pesto pasta. You'd like the service,
solicitous, not pushy. In fact,
it's that I'm crying over. Solicitude
is hard to take these days. I'm here to write,
and you're here too—in the wine, the fish,
my hurt, it's all honoring you,
including those white sails, so far off
I can't tell if they're still or moving.

A Walk after Chemo

For the moment, nothing dies.
Three days of rain, but now
sun walks the ridge, sends nine geese over,
bright and honking.
Down in the grass, barely catching
corner of a walker's eye,
something shuttles the light,
it's beating faster than wings–
the front paws of a rabbit flailing,
aware of nothing but *can't*.
Small, young, on its back.
Now I see both hind legs are bound
by stiff, wet grass, the knotted blades
so tight I panic.
Hit by a car.
Blood drips from one eye,
what good is there in my desperate
fingers? All I want
is a rabbit upright in clover
and this exultant sun in my bones.

Invitation

We guess you have asked only us
this first time, wanting a perfect match,
two couples honoring partners, then

hands across, no other figures,
no pair from up the street who will
say so much about everything

we don't want to understand—high school
football, dog snacks that control tartar, escalating
costs of fixtures for the downstairs bath.

During the long, cold drive, we hunger
for new immensities, drinks by the fire
a prelude to passionate exchanges

bypassing all civilities of job,
home, recipes, the current climate
in Washington and Wall Street,

fiber optics, even the state of
marriage nowadays, but swinging bravely
against gravity of the mundane

to search the springing flames, the figure
in the carpet, being and nothingness,
the Tao of it all. But here's

the other couple. Two kids. A dog,
a large dog. And factoids lead the dance.
Two hosts, four guests, are all

we are. Outside, the interchange
of snow and stars softly pursues
a deepening acquaintance.

Advent Lambs

These crisp December nights I coax you out
to visit, in a neighbor's shed, two lambs,
brown, woolly, peaceable.
Last year it was goats,
who licked paint off the Holy Family
and were summarily removed,
well before Christmas.

This noon I catch our neighbor in the act
of wiring epiphany—one flash, and the plaster
Virgin turns translucent.
                              I offer you
only the lambs. Last year I was pregnant
again, with cancer, my womb long gone,
dark miracle. How to remove an emptiness?
But now something leaps inside me,
as through the trees we see a glow,
and soon a fence. We're there.

Huddled far back in the shed, massed shadow
breaks apart. One lamb sidles towards us,
lipping the bundled straw. "Maaaa-aa,"
I call, and offer a handful.
                              A car pulls up
and two figures join us, silently,
small boy and mother.
I pass my straw to the child,
who sticks it out in a shaky hand.
We don't speak,
but we're a congregation.

Janet, Dying

for Winnie and Rebecca

Silly-sweet on morphine at last,
      you summon the balloons from the ceiling,
two silvery floaters. You want them tied
      to the bed. Yesterday you could have named
all five rivers of Hades; so many foreign
      kingdoms and waters know you by name.
Now you are your own stream.
      Nonsense pours from your sore mouth
to set you afloat and let your
      daughters slip, at last, tenderly, into laughter.
Do you know your babble will be the prelude
      to silence? Your current sets one way now,
and you look so like my dying mother,
      both of you stoic, witty,
soft-cheeked but gaunt with cancer,
      surrendering control with grim reluctance–
to become two hallucinating Lucies
      adrift in the marmalade, spilling diamonds
and roses, as though the fairy tales you read us
      had opened one last time to take
you in while there was still
      a wish left–and you wished for
those damned silly balloons.

Solstice Variations

for Tim, 1951-2005

The early dark is good for
the cold, is good
for feeding butter to the cat,

whose forepaws cup my finger
till he's tongued it gleaming
warm—a moment's grace

from our neighbor's dark
that birthed
a vast, inflated crèche.

The Virgin's rubber face
glows, featureless, her babe's
a swollen, swaddled lump.

No star
guides us to their
perfect light.

The dark's not deep enough
to shroud us from ourselves.
Bone-licking, it chills,

settles in my throat,
speaking
a silent name:

My brother,
who took yourself to die
on the mountain trail,

I feel you
back, sipping from
the bloody pit

of memory.
You mouth the air
but I can only dream

your laughter
puncturing
the rubber crèche,

the missing camel's
hump. Your silence
birthing the early dark.

Only in Sleep

The Lapland women
masticated deer hide till it was soft
for sewing. That was fourth-grade
geography, the year I'd hide
pieces of tough, half-gnawed
Sunday roast in my napkin,
wanting strained peaches.
Nervous that the day's events passing
over the knives and forks meant
something else.
Bedtime was safer, the reading voices
seamless, the animals speaking what was
set down for them.

In sleep now I hunger for words,
some new mother-tongue.
Did you chew it well?
I ask the scruffy-bearded cook
who might be Gary Snyder,
Sierra sutra, bent over a campfire,
shaking the blackened pan.
Is it fiddle ferns? streambed pebbles
worn smooth as an old story?
The poet tastes something.
Behind him a face in shadow, maybe
a monk waiting hopefully
for boiled coffee.
                    Snyder is silent,
his rawhide laces undone. The boots,
scarred by granite, have gone soft
and loose, but he looks like he still
has something to say,

you can almost hear the bonebox grind.
He spits on his hands,
stoops and grabs a smoldering twig,
then slowly chews it green.
Right down to the quick,
my tongue says, waking
to the taste of bark and sap.

On the Revlon Walk for Women's Cancers

Spring laces the park with leaves
and brings in the great walks
of protest against dying.

All winter, bodies have turned
on themselves, grown tumors,
grown toxic, turned

cold. Now this green weekend,
we who survive and remember
stream up from the subway.

Caged in the blast and beat of Times
Square, we elbow, slump, dance in place,
thrust signs skyward that speak

temporary alliance against death's
who do you think you are?
The great clouds of spring

mass overhead as we break free
of flesh and concrete,
as we move into the park.

Like trees, we flower. Stories
unfold: *You lose your whole self*
those days right after treatment. . . .

No one there could speak
my language. . . . She was
old so no one cared.

Who do we think we are?
We have paid in years
of gloss and cover,

filling in the cancer hollows
of cheeks, replacing lost
eyebrows. You cannot

make up a ghost.
The park goes on unfurling
glamour in goody bags of blush and liner.

Tiring, we try to release fear
to the green-filtered light–

to triumph, silently,
in one more spring.

Memento Mori

Never can I remember joy
as this dazzle.
                    My face, age two,
beams back such love for hers,
the lens between us melts.

She must have said, "Play the piano,
Rabbit, show Daddy how you play."
I stand perpendicular to the Steinway,
stiff as some figure on a tombstone,
stretching my right arm back
to press a key I find by feel
since I want to keep looking
straight into her eye and not let go
of her smile–she must have
smiled. I'm in sky-blue
overalls, but–what was she thinking?–

above me, hung from the floor lamp
like a headless ghost, here's
my party dress
without me in it.
Strangely convenient, just as if
the young she-pharaoh might
need that smocking in the afterlife.
And there, crammed high
on an end table where they don't belong,
Dolly and stuffed Lamb ride
in my birthday wagon.
                    Who knows
what burdens the infant dead may have
to pull behind them, what loneliness

will require friends. Mother was always
provident. The living room's
a burial chamber.
                    She might as well
have wrapped me, mummy-style,
in the light-blue blanket, still warm
with her and Father's smells.
I took it after their deaths,
for comfort. Now it holds
my heat and our mortality.
Looking at the snapshot I can hear
a muffled, pale-blue whisper:
                              Keep me with you.

I'll wrap your naked body
at the end.

Saint Luke's Garden, Hudson Street

The wind plays April here.
Bells and songbirds, all sway, all
open mouths, fling down glory
that cracks the earth, stirs
sun breath to slip between
these brick walls and nest
in magnolia virginiana, heart
of our contemplation. Praise
the silver underside of its leaves.

Who's here to learn nesting?
That sparrow tugs a clump of pale grass
twice his size, stiff relic of winter,
another pecks string off some rose canes,
and over there a wren plucks
at her own breast.
              We five or six strangers,
each having found a half-concealed
bench, are silent. Maybe woolgathering,
lost in the anthem, heedless
of the offering plate.
              Or kneeling inwardly
in silent cry. My body's a nest
for cancer. Green, green, flows around me.
Beaks open, and the wind shows silver.
Tomorrow's surgery will pluck
and bleed me of cells that spring
called back, that something in me
wanted just as much as these creamy blossoms
want light. Some green bell tolled and woke
what I thought dead.
              I'm here

to learn all over what to ask for.
April floods the ear, confuses
breathing, but I know
this garden's mine, an hour's train ride
into city miracle of pomegranate,
fig, rosemary, walled by a church
two hundred years ago. All praise,
miracle of pawpaw, of Asian Pear,
fleur-de-lis, Cedar of Lebanon,
and *rose bracteata*, "the mermaid."
Lists are steadying, but *laude*
harrows the whole mouth, delicate touch
of tongue back to the painful
throat howl. Wall and wind
muffle the traffic here. Tomorrow
I'll be on a highway south,
then flat out loss, no time,
no breath, no mind.
                    How can we live
closed and open? Tradition says
look to the sparrow.
                    Tug, crack, fling,
I pray my shell and core,
petal and fuse. Tell me the moment
the mix is right. Whoever I am then
will squat down in herself and turn
and turn, shaping the nest again.

I Take the Brahms Third Symphony to My MRI

for Bill

It's all about breath—winds, brass,
even the strings. The man in scrubs
does his work with dye and needles,
then slides me into the coffin's
tube of gray light. I check myself:
metal off, IV taped,
arms over the head, torso
strapped down, sheet pulled
up to the chin. Music on.

Already I'm thinking, soft,
too soft. After the first crash
of wind chords and the strings' brief
passionato, heroic falling theme
that can't decide if it's major or minor,
Brahms dies fast to a whisper
of clarinet. Nothing's resolved,
even downbeats lose themselves,
stress without measure.

But what music could cut
this machine's drill and blast
and the instructing voice, "Take a deep breath
and hold it."
                I try to think about my
instrument, hold a long note,
enter the beat of Toscanini's mind as he
fathoms Brahms.
                "Breathe now,
relax." I expel air as the flutes drift back,

breathe silver. My protons move
deep in my liver, deep in their atoms of
hydrogen they shift, magnetic dance
to a drill, pound, blast that breaks
the music's meaning.

Still, memory tries to hear
what's missing. Must be somewhere
in the *andante*, second theme, bassoon,
dolce, dolce, how can breath travel
through all that coiled wood in time
to speak with the clarinet, and softly, too.

In the finale—if I'm released by then—
we'll drive as far as need be just to finish.
We'll hear that theme again, haunting a storm
of trombones. Fragments from the whole
past hour will gather to return us home
or beyond home.

How things recur—tests, cancer,
breath, this 1950's concert
willed to us by my dead brother.
I hear him listening.
I know the cello line through
bow arm and fingers, inhaling
a child memory of Brahms, a trio
in summer by a lake.
                    "Breathe in. . . and hold it."
Inside the metal skin of blast, test, fear,
the music must be going on. . . somewhere.

Reviewing the Skull

"Good bones," you say, sizing up my skull
with an artist's eye. If bones can blush,
under this hairless scalp, mine do.
We've just met, you and the bones,
I forget your name, but you make
        book art
                and baskets.
As you read a face,
do you alter it? Shift of planes and plates,
inspire   unspell

If you rewove this bone-bag–
thrum of chemo through neural mesh,
cauliflower, spill and gather, skull's toxic flag–
what might it bear?

riverweed floats a baby. . .
      from husk of cornsilks. . . the naked crown
           top of the head taken off
              a skylight
                  a poem
                      a death

A tisket, a tasket,

        a green and yellow basket

    I wrote a letter to my love,

        and on the way I lost it

Scatbrainsong:

                is this where I take

   my text?

where mind's at home
            whatever
                the omen

take the thought of my hair

make a shirt to wear

wherever it's gone

        but praise, yes, praise

        the bones

        the good bones

        bared

About the Author

Judy Rowe Michaels is poet in residence, English teacher, and coordinator of the Lively Arts program at Princeton Day School and a poet in the schools for the Geraldine R. Dodge Foundation. Her first poetry collection, *The Forest of Wild Hands*, was published by University Press of Florida, and her poems have appeared in such journals as *Poetry, Poetry Northwest, The Women's Review of Books, Columbia, English Journal, Nimrod International Journal, CALYX, River Styx,* and *Kalliope.* She has won two poetry fellowships from the New Jersey State Council on the Arts and is a member of a central New Jersey critique and performance group, Cool Women. Author of two books on teaching writing to high school students, she presents regularly at conferences. She earned her B.A. with honors in English from Middlebury College and her Ph.D. from Bryn Mawr.

A five-time ovarian cancer patient, she participates in the program Survivors Speaking to Students, which is in sixty medical schools around the country and is sponsored by the Ovarian Cancer National Alliance. Having grown up in New England, she now lives with her husband, Bill, and Maine Coon Cat, Galway, on a ridge of the Sourland Mountains in New Jersey but also shares a summer cabin in Maine with her sister and brothers.

Breinigsville, PA USA
12 February 2010
232400BV00001B/8/P